Introducing the Shakers

ABOUT THE COVER

The illustration on the front cover depicts not only a typi
Shaker brother and a Shaker sister, but also a Shaker sid
chair with candle-flame finial, and checkerboard seat
created by crosslapped cloth tapes. The gambrel roof on
the building was commonly found on Shaker meeting
houses. The picture was painted by William A. Kuhlman
a free-lance illustrator with a studio in Perrysburg, Ohio.
Mr. Kuhlman has created award-winning designs and ill
trations for both print and film media.

ABOUT THE AUTHOR

Diana Van Kolken was introduced to the Shaker story
in 1969 when she and her husband, Paul, were living in
Watervliet, New York, and they came upon the Shaker
cemetery in which Mother Ann Lee is buried. Their inte
est increased with visits to other Shaker sites. Later the V
Kolkens returned to their native Michigan where Pa
became city editor of the Holland *Sentinel*. In 1978 they p
chased a small paper called *The World of Shaker*, changed
its name to *The Shaker Messenger*, and built it into a maga
zine of news and information for Shaker enthusiasts. Today
Diana operates a store in Holland, Mich. devoted to Shaker
and folk art, lectures on the Shakers and represents crafts-
people at country folk art shows. *(Photo by Louis Schakel)*

Introducing the Shakers
An Explanation and Directory

Diana Van Kolken

General Editor: James H. Bissland III
Designed by Lynn Hostetler

Gabriel's Horn Publishing Co.
Bowling Green, Ohio

Gabriel's Horn Publishing Co.
P.O. Box 141
Bowling Green, Ohio 43402

Printed in the United States of America

10 09 08 07 06 05 04 03 02   15 14 13 12 11 10
ISBN 0-911861-04-1

Contents

Introducing the Shakers

The United Society of Believers in Christ's Second Appearing, better known as "the Shakers," is America's oldest communal society.

For over two hundred years its members have lived quietly in secluded communities, sharing a simple life and seeking perfection in everything they do, from cooking to carpentry.

Dedicated to the glory of God, Shaker perfectionism can be seen in the serene beauty of their villages, in the gracefulness of their furniture and crafts, and in their qualities of character — devotion, thrift, humanity, ingenuity.

America is a land of pioneers, dreamers and idealists, who dared to explore new frontiers and to create a new society. The Shakers were spiritual pioneers, and when we look at them, we see something of ourselves. The Shakers are not simply one important chapter in the American saga; in their quest, they are a symbol of it.

The Shakers have been part of the American scene since 1774, and have been fascinating writers and observers, foreign and domestic, ever since. Nor have the Shakers themselves been shy about publishing their beliefs, history, music and industry.

In the twentieth century, popular interest in the Shakers has accelerated even as their numbers have continued to decline. One after another, museums and libraries have begun collections; from Maine to Kentucky work goes on to restore and preserve Shaker sites. Shaker furniture and crafts are avidly sought by collectors of Americana. Each year brings more books, magazine articles, films and conferences about the Shakers.

And yet, for many people, there are still questions. Why are they called Shakers? Are they related to the Quakers or the Amish? Why have they lasted so long — and why have their numbers declined? Why are they celibate? And so on.

Each of these questions has been discussed at length in books by and about the Shakers. The book you are now holding does not attempt to be so comprehensive. It is merely an introduction for the first-time inquirer.

Nevertheless, it is hoped that this little book will give you a greater appreciation for those men and women who called themselves Shakers and who contributed so much to the American experience.

A directory of the most commonly visited Shaker sites is included for those who wish to see where the Shakers put their "hands to work and their hearts to God."

Introducing the Shakers

1. Why are they called Shakers?

The early Shakers, some of whom may have been members at one time of the Religious Society of Friends, or Quakers, would become excited during their meetings in England in the mid-1700s. In their ecstasy, the worshippers would whirl and tremble, "shaking" off sins and evil. Startled onlookers called them "Shaking Quakers," or "Shakers."

Originally, the name "Shaker" was used in derision. But within a few years, the very people it had been used to mock adopted it as their own.

For much of its history, the sect's members have referred to themselves both formally and informally as Shakers, although the full name for their order is The United Society of Believers in Christ's Second Appearing.

Shakers also refer to themselves as "Believers," and their sect as "The United Society."

Over the years, the ecstatic shaking that gave the sect its name evolved into more ritualized dancing. Shaker services have also included traditional worship forms, such as singing, meditation and prayer.

Still, 19th-century Americans regarded dancing as a peculiar worship form, and Shaker services attracted many spectators. A traveler in 1831 told of arriving at a Shaker service in Shirley, Massachusetts, to find "a large number of carriages of various kinds ranged along the fence, most of them from neighboring towns, but some from considerable distance, and all freighted with curious visitors."

Today, recreations of Shaker dancing occasionally may be seen at museums and festivals of people interested in the Shakers. Modern spectators find the dances beautiful and inspiring.

2. Are the Shakers like the Quakers and the Amish?

The Shakers, Quakers, and Amish people share some similarities — and also some major differences.

All are Christians who strive to live their faiths. All are pacificists, gentle and humane; all are nonmatrialistic, favoring — at least in tradition — "plainness" in dress and lifestyle. All opposed slavery; all have profound respect for the land and nature's resources. Both the Shakers and the Amish withdrew from the world to live in their own communities. In some ways, therefore, these three religious groups may seem to be very much the same.

But they are not. The Quakers developed primarily in England. While there were some Quaker influences on the Shakers in their earliest years in England, the Shakers primarily grew out of American revivalist and separatist movements. And the Amish derived from the tradition of post-Reformation German radical pietism.

The Quakers, Shakers and Amish differ theologically. They also differ in the way they live. Unlike the Shakers and Amish, Quakers do not live in their own communities. Unlike the Amish and the Quakers, the Shakers are celibate and do not marry, relying on conversion for new members. Unlike the Amish also, the Shakers believe in full equality of the sexes.

In this technological age, another difference between the Shakers and Amish is especially interesting. The Amish, as well as certain other Mennonite sects in varying degrees, reject most modern technology.

The Shakers, on the other hand, have always embraced modern technology. In years past, for example, many Shaker communities had running water and electricity before their more worldly neighbors. Shakers eagerly read the latest scientific journals and applied their findings to matters of agriculture, health, and manufacturing. A number of inventions and innovations have been attributed to the ingenious Shakers.

3. How did Shakerism start?

England in the mid-1700s was a land of sweeping change — and popular unrest.

Almost endless war with Spain and France had brought hardship and taxation to the people. The Industrial Revolution was emptying the countryside and turning cities like Manchester into crowded, smoky mill towns. Religious agitators like John Wesley and George Whitefield were stirring crowds of ordinary people who yearned for a change from the Anglican Church, the official church of England.

The time was ripe for new religious sects. One of them was born about 1747 in Bolton-on-Moors, a grimy little town near Manchester. Here a small group of religious dissenters came into being under the guidance of two Quaker tailors, Jane and James Wardley.

The Wardleys left the Quakers. They may have done so — although this is un-proven — under the influence of a radical sect of French Calvinists known as the "Prophets."

The "Prophets" were living in exile in England, where they were generally despised for their fanaticism and bizarre behavior.

The Wardleys had no clearly formulated doctrine of their own. Instead, they were anti-clerical, apocalyptic, and millenial in their beliefs. They warned all who listen to "amend your lives. Repent. For the kingdom of God is at hand."

Like Quakers, followers of the Wardleys might begin a meeting in silent meditation. But then, like the "French Prophets," they might be seized with "a mighty trembling, under which they would express the indignation of God against all sin. At other times they were affected . . . with a mighty shaking . . . " Members of the congregation "occasionally exercised in singing, shouting, or walking the floor, under the influence of spiritual signs, shoving each other about."

"Mother Jane" Wardley warned that when Christ appeared, "all anti-Christian denominations — the priests, the church, the pope — will be swept away." She was referring, of course, to Anglican as well as Roman Catholic churches.

Not surprisingly, most of the Wardleys' neighbors viewed them with suspicion and dislike. But it was to this little group that in September, 1758, that a young woman from Manchester was attracted. Her name was Ann Lees. Later she was to become known as Mother Ann Lee, the driving force behind Shakerism.

4. Who was Mother Ann Lee?

Ann Lees, later shortened to Lee, was
born in England on February 29, 1736.
She was the second of eight children of
John Lees, a blacksmith who added to his
income by tailoring. The Lees family lived
in Toad Lane (now Todd Street) in the mill
city of Manchester.

Little is known of Ann's childhood,
although she is said to have had spiritual
yearnings from an early age and to have told
her mother that she had "visions of angels."
Ann had no schooling and was soon sent to
work in a textile mill. At about age 20 she
was working as a cook in a public infirmary.

In 1758, at age 22, she joined a little sect
of religious dissenters led by Jane and James
Wardley. The Wardleys and their followers
were preaching that the kingdom of God was
at hand. In the ecstasy of their worship, they
sometimes shook or trembled violently.

At first, Ann Lees did not play a major
role in the Wardley society. But in 1762 she
was married — against her
will, it is said —
to a Manchester
blacksmith
named
Abraham

Standerin (or Stanley). Ann was a serious young woman, struggling with religious questions; Standerin, on the other hand, was a "kindly man who loved his beef and beer, his chimney corner and seat in village tavern."

Tragedy followed: one after another, in difficult deliveries, Ann bore four children, three of whom died in infancy, the fourth after lingering a few years. Deeply troubled and in broken health, she struggled to purify herself, ultimately experiencing a complete conversion. "My soul broke forth to God," she said.

With new zeal and restored health, she was soon taking a more active part in the Wardley society, speaking out especially against "cohabitation of the sexes." The sect's moral and discipline sharpened; its criticism of the established church grew more outspoken, and its membership larger, coming to include even Ann's father and younger brother, William.

The meetings grew so loud, and the anger of mobs opposed to them so violent, that authorities were summoned several times. In 1772 and again in 1773, according to old records, "Ann Lees a shaker" and others were arrested. Ann was imprisoned for several weeks; on her release, she told of having had a vision of Christ. The other "Shakers" saw in the martyred Ann the fulfillment of the prophesy of the second coming of Christ.

"I am Ann the Word," the charismatic young woman said; the other members of the sect acknowledged her now as their leader by giving her the title of "Mother."

5. How did Shakerism come to America?

The Shakers were persecuted in England and prevented from preaching in public. But they saw visions of a chosen people waiting in New England. In the spring of 1774 Mother Ann, her husband, and seven followers (not including the Wardleys, who had left the society) sailed for America aboard the ship *Mariah*.

It was not an easy voyage. The captain grew angry with the Shakers' singing and dancing, and threatened to throw them overboard. When a heavy wave struck the *Mariah* and loosened a plank, threatening to sink the ship, Mother Ann told the despairing captain she had had a vision they would be saved. Just then another wave forced the loose plank back in place, saving the *Mariah*.

The Shakers arrived in New York harbor on August 6, 1774. Some of the party went up the Hudson River to Albany to look for land, while others separated to find work. Ann found a job doing laundry, but left it to nurse her husband, who had become seriously ill in the late summer of 1775.

After Abraham's recovery, he began to lead a life of debauchery, punctuated by demands that Ann end her celibacy. She refused, and Abraham left to live with a "lewd woman." So ended 13 years of unhappy marriage.

Meanwhile, an advance party of Shakers had found and settled land in Niskeyuna — known as Watervliet today — about seven or eight miles from Albany. A log cabin, with separate quarters for brethren and sisters, was built, and crops begun. Mother Ann joined the settlement in 1776, and the next three years were spent improving the little community on the New York frontier.

Their hardscrabble existence and a failure to attract new members were deeply discouraging to the pioneer Shakers. Still preaching that the converts "will come like doves," however, Mother Ann continued to hold the little group together in the wilderness.

About this time, religious revivals were sweeping the land. One, a New Light Baptist revival under the leadership of Joseph Meacham, was occurring at New Lebanon, New York, and Hancock, Massachusetts. Meacham and others heard of the preaching at Niskeyuna and were attracted to it; before long, he and many of his congregation as well as other societies in the area, were converted to Shakerism.

By now the American Revolution was underway, and the Shakers' pacifism brought them under suspicion. In 1780 Mother Ann was imprisoned for treason and held in jail for half a year until her followers convinced the governor of her innocence. The experience only enchanced Mother Ann's fame, however, and soon the Shakers were planning a missionary trip to New England.

6. How widely did Shakerism spread?

From 1781 to 1783, Ann Lee and a small party of followers, called elders, went on a missionary trip through eastern New York, Massachusetts and Connecticut. They visited 36 towns where Shaker converts lived, laying foundations for a number of Shaker villages that would arise later.

These pioneer Shakers faced suspicion and mobs wherever they went, but kept on gaining converts. In Harvard, Massachusetts, a hamlet about 25 miles northwest of Boston, they set up eastern headquarters. Here they bought the ''Square House,'' where another prophet, Shadrach Ireland, had lived and died, and inherited many of his followers.

New members were attracted to meetings at the Square House. The Shakers also made side trips to nearby villages. Their growth was marred by attacks of ruffians, but the Shakers survived and their tormentors — according to tradition — fell into poverty and other bad ends.

In 1784, a year after her return to Niskeyuna, Mother Ann died at age 48. The beatings, hard travel, strenuous preaching and years of privation had exacted their price.

Leadership of the sect went to James Whitaker, under whose orders a meeting house at New Lebanon, New York, was raised in 1785, leading to the first fully established community in 1787. Then followed a succession of leaders, many of them so strong that they commanded great respect from outsiders.

Starting with New Lebanon in 1787, the Shakers began withdrawing from the world to form their own communities. Property was donated to the order by new members; communal dwellings were built; and elders, deacons and trustees were appointed. Industries were begun.

By 1794, eleven eastern communities had been established in New York, Massachusetts, New Hampshire, Connecticut and Maine. When the Shakers learned of a religious revival on what was then America's western frontier, they sent out missionaries, starting in 1805. From them would come major communities in Ohio and Kentucky.

In all, 18 major Shaker communities eventually were organized, as well as six shorter lived ones located as far south as Florida and as far west as Indiana.

At its height in the 1850s, the Shaker movement had an estimated 6,000 members in self-supporting communities from Maine to Kentucky.

7. What are the basic tenets of Shakerism?

Shakers believe that God appears and speaks to and through people, who are His church. And, like the early Christians, the Shakers believe in universal love: "Thou shall love they neighbor as thyself."

Among the basic tenets of Shakerism are celibacy, separation from the world, communal sharing of goods, confessions of sins, equality of the sexes, and pacifism.

CELIBACY: From the beginning, Ann Lee had condemned cohabitation, reminding her listeners that lust had resulted in Man's expulsion from the Garden of Eden. Like Mother Ann, Shakers dedicated themselves to lives of purity, giving up exclusive relationships and living together in families as brothers and sisters.

Naturally, outsiders demanded: "What would become of the world if all became Shakers?" The Shakers replied there was no danger of that, for God had allowed for "two orders of humanity," one expected to reproduce itself, while the other — the Shakers — dedicated themselves to the Lord's work. The Shakers were also apt to wryly observe that

"in view of the condition of a good part of the people in it . . . it might not be a bad idea to let the world run out."

SEPARATION FROM THE WORLD: From the late 1700s until the present, Shakers have lived in their own communities, a practice that shielded them from some of the less wholesome influences of mainstream society but also made them objects of curiosity. Shakers have differed among themselves as to how severe the separation should be; the great Shaker leader Frederick Evans, for example, was an ardent public spokesman in the 1800s for various social reforms, scientific agriculture and sanitation; some other Shaker leaders of the time opposed such participation in the world's affairs.

SHARING OF GOODS: It was share and share alike among the Shakers. All converts turned over their property — from large farms to the simplest tools — to the society when they joined it. No member held "even a dollar of property" for his own use.

CONFESSION OF SINS: Each new convert confessed his or her sins to an elder or eldress and at specified times thereafter.

EQUALITY: Shakers believed in equality for all people regardless of race or sex. Equality between males and females was believed to be God's will at the creation. And blacks were welcomed into the society.

PACIFISM: Like the Quakers, the Shakers were conscientious objectors to war, and refused to serve in wars ranging from the Revolution to the Civil War, although their objections frequently brought them persecution.

8. If the Shakers didn't marry, how did they expect to grow?

The handful of pioneer Shakers who came to America in 1774 swelled into a society with an estimated 6,000 members by the mid-1800s. During those years, the order's growth came primarily from converts spurred by revival fever.

Sometimes whole families would join, providing the Shakers with children. On joining, these families were separated, with the children coming under the care of the Shaker family as a whole and the mother and father beginning lives of celibacy as ''brother'' and ''sister.''

While this may seem harsh to us today, the atmosphere in a Shaker village was a loving one. Shaker rules could be strict, but were tempered by humanity.

As revivalism declined, so did Shaker membership, but some people continued to find the Shaker faith attractive and join for religious reasons.

Many orphans were taken in and given kindly care by the Shakers. Sometimes

children were sent to the Shakers to attend school or learn a trade. On reaching young adulthood, some would take Shaker vows themselves, although they were never pressured to do so.

Women who had no families or means of support in the outside world would come to the Shaker villages where they would find security and equality. For some, celibate life was a release from marriage and fear of childbirth.

Families who had fallen on hard times would move in with the Shakers, although many of these "winter Shakers," as they were called, would leave when times got better.

And the Shakers themselves made certain efforts to enlist new members, although they were careful to pressure no one. Their meeting houses were open to the curious. They issued many pamphlets and books explaining their faith. From 1871 to 1899, they published a monthly periodical, commonly referred to as *The Manifesto*, which artfully blended discussions of Shaker religious beliefs with agricultural and household hints, music and poetry. *The Manifesto*, it was explained, was to serve as "our principal missionary."

9. How did the Shakers organize and govern themselves?

A Shaker village or local society consisted of brothers and sisters, each highly self-sufficient.

In their peak years, each family might have 50 to 100 members, although in the earlier and later years of Shakerism many families were smaller.

The brothers and sisters of a family would live in a dwelling house that provided separate doorways, stairs and sleeping accommodations for the sexes. The dwelling house would have its own kitchens and dining rooms, weekday meeting room, and sometimes an infirmary.

Each family usually had its own gardens, crops, livestock, outbuildings, workshops, and, in a few cases, a schoolhouse. Families would often have their own store or trustees' building where visitors were welcomed and goods sold to the "world's people."

Covenanted Shakers — those who had dedicated all they possessed to the Order and had fully entered the Shaker way of life — would live in the Center or Church Family, sometimes called the Senior Order.

Families who wished to experience Shaker life but who were not ready to make a full commitment would live in the Novitiate Order, and persons having no family ties would live in the Junior Order.

These orders and other covenanted families in a local Shaker society were often named according to their geographical relationship to the Church or Center Family: North Family, South Family, and so on. Sometimes families were named by the work in which they specialized (Mill Family or Brickyard Family), and sometimes they were designated by number, such as First Family or Second Family.

In the center of the entire Shaker village would be a meeting house at which all families worshipped on Sunday. Families might also share a schoolhouse and certain other facilities, such as barns or shops.

Each of the families was governed by two elders and two eldresses, who oversaw the spiritual needs of the members. The family also had deacons and deaconesses to manage the daily work of the family.

When business with the outside world began to warrant it, trustees were selected and given the responsibility for the family's finances and business transactions with the world's people.

The elders and eldresses of the Church or Center Family oversaw the village or local society as a whole. Sometimes several societies were united under one ministry called the "bishopric." At the top was the New Lebanon, New York, ministry, which from the beginning was considered the governing body of the entire Shaker sect. Usually this head or lead ministry had four elders and eldresses, of whom the leading elder might be called "Father" and the leading eldress "Mother."

10. How did the Shakers earn their living?

From the beginning, the Shakers tried to make their communities as self-sufficient as possible. In the early years, they typically suffered great hardships and barely eked out an existence, but through hard work, ingenuity and concern for scientific methods, were gradually able to begin producing surpluses for sale to the outside world.

Farm surpluses and herbal products brought the Shakers their first outside income. The "kitchen industries" produced dried sweet corn, apples, applesauce, jam and preserves.

A wide variety of medicinal herbs were raised, processed and sold through pharmaceutical companies. The Shakers seem to have entered the herb business in a limited way around 1800, and more substantially around 1820. During this period the Shakers also started getting into the garden seed business; within a few years Shaker peddlers were marketing them on regular routes from New England to the South.

The Shakers developed the flat household broom we know today, and made its production a major industry. Brushes, wooden ware (such as baskets, tubs, barrels and pails), clay pipes, rug whips and pens were also manufactured in the shops of the Believers.

Shaker sisters wove cloth, straw bonnets, carpets, fans and baskets. They knitted and

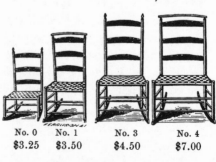

| No. 0 | No. 1 | No. 3 | No. 4 |
| $3.25 | $3.50 | $4.50 | $7.00 |

sewed, the famous Shaker "Dorothy cloak" being one of their products.

Shaker brothers manufactured spinning wheels, swifts, oval boxes, and chairs. Indeed, the making of chairs with their delicate, carefully proportioned lines, became one of their most notable industries. Shakers first began making chairs for sale in the late 1700s, and may have been the first chair manufacturers in the country.

Commercial chairmaking continued sporadically, but in 1852, the Shakers at New Lebanon, New York, settled down to making and selling chairs in large quantities. They issued catalogs of stools, straight chairs, and rocking chairs in ranges of sizes designated by number, from "0" to "7." These chairs are sought by modern collectors of Americana who prize them for their simple grace and fine workmanship.

Today, the Shaker community at Sabbathday Lake, Maine, still raises sheep and sells the wool. Handmade items and tins of herbs and teas, surplus from their garden, are sold in their shop.

As in all things, the Shakers did not work for private gain but for the good of the society. And in everything the Shakers did commercially, they became famed for their industriousness, efficiency, honesty, and concern for selling only the best. Throughout nineteenth-century America, "Shaker made" was a synonym for quality.

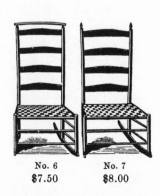

No. 6   No. 7
$7.50 $8.00   23

11. Was it all work and no play for the Shakers?

Life was hard for the Shakers in the earliest years, and certainly work was always a major part of Shaker life. Making work less burdensome, however, was the Believers' attitude toward it: it was dedicated to God's purposes and therefore holy. In addition, the Shakers worked together and shared the heaviest tasks. Individuals were also given the kinds of work they did best, and chores were rotated, giving the day some variety.

Also providing a change of pace were various seasonal tasks: cornhusking, nut and berry gathering, maple syrup collecting and sugar making.

In addition, Shakers enjoyed such diversions as picnics, fishing, hiking, sleigh and carriage rides. Many Shaker communities had recreation areas like Hemlock Grove at North Union, Ohio (now the Cleveland suburb of Shaker Heights). This was described as "a splendid grove of native hemlock" on the border of Doan Brook and Lower Lake where the Shakers could go strolling and hold picnics.

Singing was a major source of entertainment for the Shakers, and in later years musical instruments became popular. In later years the Shakers also enjoyed staging of plays or pageants during holiday seasons such as Christmas.

It would be a mistake to think of the Shakers as grim individuals who unsmilingly went about their days of work and worship. While they had no taste for many of the world's diversions, they also enjoyed wholesome pleasures of their own, and were quite capable of humor, sometimes at their own expense.

12. Did Shakers pay taxes, join the army, or vote?

The Shakers did not try to avoid paying most kinds of taxes. They willingly paid the equivalent of local property taxes without seeking exemption as a religious organization.

Sometimes, however, they did object to certain kinds of taxes which they considered unfair or morally wrong, such as parish taxes, taxes to support war efforts, or taxes that were discriminatory.

In addition to paying most taxes, Shakers donated labor and money for public roads and bridges, and gave relief to the poor and the hungry who appeared at their gates, sometimes to the point of causing hardship to themselves. Donations were sent to Ireland during the potato famine.

As pacifists, Shakers sought exemption from military duty. In their early history they sometimes were persecuted and imprisoned for this, but later were able to obtain exemptions as conscientious objectors. Sometimes they were able to substitute public service for militia duty.

The great Shaker elder, Frederick Evans, was a formidable personality and widely respected among the "world's people." During the Civil War he approached President Lincoln with a petition for exemption of Shakers from military draft. Lincoln granted the petition, while telling Evans admiringly, "You ought to be made to fight. We need regiments of just such men as you."

The Kentucky Shaker societies suffered heavily from the incursions of Civil War armies. Nevertheless, the southern Believers ministered impartially to the soldiers of both sides, feeding, housing and nursing the armies whenever they camped on Shaker property.

Abstaining from politics, the Shakers did not vote, campaign, or hold office, except in rare instances. This did not mean Shakers were necessarily silent on public issues; some, such as Evans, spoke out in lectures and through the press on issues ranging from public education to the banking system.

13. What do the Shakers think about the "World's People"?

Very early in their history the Shakers withdrew from the world to live in their own communities. Certainly many of their beliefs and practices, from celibacy to community of goods, were at odds with the "world's people," as they called their non-Shaker neighbors.

Nevertheless, Shakers neither sneered at the rest of the world nor cut off relationships with it. Instead, they came to practical accommodation with their neighbors while clearly preserving their own identity.

Shaker gates were open to worldly visitors, as they are today, and through the years visitors in a steady stream have passed through the communities of the Believers.

The Shakers had good reason to stay in touch with the rest of the world, of course. From that world they obtained their converts. In it, they found markets for the goods. And from it they learned the scientific advances in agriculture and other sciences which they applied so eagerly to their own practices.

At the same time, the Shakers also gave to the outside world: most of their many inventions were never patented, and their generosity to the needy was well known.

Moreover, the Shakers realized their way of life was not for everyone. Unlike some groups who believe theirs is the only way, the Shakers felt God had created two orders of humanity, one of the world's people and another of the spiritually pure.

Confident in their own beliefs, the Shakers feel they have chosen the best way of life and do not fret over converting everyone else in the world. In the past they performed missionary work, but they never hectored candidates for conversion, insisting anyone who joined them do so with free will and full knowledge of what they were doing.

Shakers have always felt the way of life they chose was the best one. Being a Shaker not only meant a righteous life, dedicated to God's work, but also one in a busy community of sharing and love. Nineteenth-century Shakers were fond of pointing to the longevity of their members, which they considered evidence of a wholesome lifestyle.

Shakers past and present feel their beliefs and way of life challenge the ''world's people'' to strive for perfection in their own lives.

NOTICE.

In consequence of the increasing amount of company to which we are at all times subject, it becomes necessary to adopt the following

RULES FOR VISITORS.

FIRST. We wish it to be understood that we do not keep a Public House, and wish to have our Rules attended to as much as any one would the rules of their own private dwelling.

SECOND. Those who call to see their Friends or Relatives, are to visit them at the Office, and not to go elsewhere, except by permission of those in care at the office.

THIRD. Those who live near and can call at their own convenience are not expected to stay more than a few hours; but such as live at a great distance, or cannot come often, and have near relatives here, can stay from one to four days, according to circumstances. This we consider sufficient time, as a general rule.

FOURTH. All Visitors are requested to rise to take Breakfast at half past Six in the Summer, and half past Seven in the Winter.

FIFTH. At the Table we wish all to be as free as at home, but we dislike the wasteful habit of leaving food on the plate. No vice is with us the less ridiculous for being in fashion.

SIXTH. Married Persons tarrying with us over night, are respectfully notified that each sex occupy separate sleeping apartments while they remain. This rule will not be departed from under any circumstances.

SEVENTH. Strangers calling for meals or lodging are expected to pay if accommodated.

UNITED SOCIETY,

14. What was daily life like for the Shakers?

Each day the Shakers rose early to the sound of a bell. Usually they rose between 4 and 5 a.m. during the summer and an hour later in the winter.

After a few moments of kneeling in silent prayer, the sisters assigned to the kitchen would begin the first meal of the day. Other sisters would begin the household tasks of making beds and cleaning up rooms.

Meanwhile, the brothers would be tending to chores in the barns or laying out the day's work in the village's workshops.

Another ringing of the bell announced breakfast at about 6 or 7 a.m., depending on the time of the year. All would assemble for a time of meditation and then, on signal, move into the dining room in single file, taking their places at long tables. After silent prayer they would eat their meal in silence.

After breakfast, sisters not taking a turn in the kitchen went to the laundry, dairy, spin house, kitchen garden or other household industry. Brothers went to the

fields, barns and workshops where such products as chairs and brooms were manufactured for sale to the world.

Elders and eldresses usually lived and
ate apart from the family, and had their own
workshops.

Just before 12 o'clock the bell would give
the signal for the noon dinner.

Afternoons were spent doing assigned
tasks until supper, a lighter meal served
about 6 o'clock.

After supper, certain tasks might be
finished up and then the brothers and sisters
would withdraw to gatherings in their
separate retiring rooms. During these
meetings various topics of family and community interest might be discussed. The
latest scientific developments in agriculture,
health and the household arts were popular-
subjects. News from other communities by
way of letters or visitors would be heard.

These meetings also offered an oppor-
tunity for additional worship, and dances and
songs might be practiced for the community
meeting on Sunday.

Union meetings between brothers and
sisters were also held during weekday even-
ings. On these occasions the Shaker brothers
and sisters would sit facing each other from a
distance of a few feet. They might converse
on topics of similar interest or sing. Later
they would share refreshments.

Bedtime typically came at about 9 p.m.
in winter and 10 p.m. in summer.

15. What did the Shakers eat?

The early Shakers struggled to survive. At times they only had thin porridge to eat. When they had bread, it sometimes was cut and buttered before being brought to the table, so all would have equal portions. Some Sundays became fast days because of a lack of food.

But an influx of members, addition of fertile land, and diligence by the Shakers themselves began paying rewards. Their tables grew bounteous, and soon there were surpluses which could be sold to non-Believers.

Shaker cooking and good food became synonymous, and remain so to this day. In fact, the "New American Cuisine" of the 1980s, with its emphasis on healthful ingredients and wholesome, natural flavors and colors, has been traced back to the Shaker cooking of the 1800s.

A Cincinnati woman who dined at New Lebanon, New York, wrote in 1888 about her experience:

"I will simply say that I never understood before to what perfection the art of cooking can be brought. Now, I want you to get my exact meaning. There was nothing 'rich' about the meal in the English or French sense; it was 'plain' cooking made delicious to the palate, tempting to the eye, and, as we found, in the highest degree digestible and nutritious."

TABLE MONITOR.

GATHER UP THE FRAGMENTS THAT REMAIN, THAT NOTHING BE LOST.—Christ.

Here then is the pattern
 Which Jesus has set;
And his good example
 We can not forget:
With thanks for his blessings
 His word we'll obey;
But on this occasion
 We've somewhat to say.

We wish to speak plainly
 And use no deceit;

Tho' Heaven has bless'd us
 With plenty of food:
Bread, butter, and honey,
 And all that is good;
We loathe to see mixtures
 Where gentle folks dine,
Which scarcely look fit
 For the poultry or swine.

We often find left,
 On the same china dish,
Meat, apple-sauce, pickle,
 ... and minc'd fish;

The Shaker economy was based primarily on agriculture, so Shaker cooks had an aray of fresh fruits and vegetables on which to draw. Fine dairy herds and flocks of poultry provided the kitchen sisters with fresh eggs, butter and cream in abundance.

Shakers worked hard during the day and spent many other hours in worship, including dance. Good food, well prepared and in abundance, was considered essential. Accord--ingly, considerable attention was paid to the latest scientific findings about nutrition. Cooking for large numbers also meant being scientific about weights and measures of ingredients. Herbs were used liberally, and special diets devised for the infirm and elderly.

Being resourceful and thrifty people, the Shakers saved the nutritious "pot liquor" in which vegetables had been cooked and used it in sauces and soups. They denounced the milling of wheat to produce white flour and urged the use of whole grains. For a time they discouraged consumption of meat.

Many labor-saving devices were invented for use in Shaker kitchens: apple peelers and corers, pea shellers, butter workers, churns, a potato washing machine, a revolving oven that could hold sixty pies at a time.

Shaker kitchens had running water, great stone sinks, and ample storage space. And as they were throughout their villages, the Shakers were spotless housekeepers in the kitchen.

While the Shakers urged those who sat at their tables to eat heartily, Believers and visitors alike were reminded to "Shaker their plates," meaning no food was to be left on them. So there would be no misunderstanding, a printed set of rules, called the "Table Monitor," was hung in the dining rooms.

16. How did the Shakers dress?

Shaker men were primarily farmers and artisans, and Shaker women industrious workers in kitchens and workshops. Shaker doctrine stressed simplicity, plainness and modesty. For many years, therefore, Shaker dress tended to reflect these qualities, although styles did change.

In the very earliest years, the Shakers wore the clothing they brought into the community. Later, dress codes prescribed strict uniformity in color, material and style, so as to achieve a sense of equality and community and prevent jealousies.

Though plain, Shaker clothing was of high quality and intended for long use. Various garments were specified for work, everyday, or Sunday wear. Every garment was marked with the user's initials, and great care was taken in the proper cleaning, mending and storage of clothing. Shakers believed in keeping everything in its proper place, as the number of cupboards, drawers and storerooms in every Shaker dwelling house demonstrates.

For some years early in Shaker history, sisters wore butternut-dyed worsted long gowns and checked aprons to winter Sabbath services, and light-colored short sleeve gowns over petticoats to summer services.

White neck cloths were adopted, evolving into the "berthas," or wide round collars covering the shoulders. The sisters eventually adopted long dresses with pleated skirts. Sisters wore small white caps and straw or palm leaf bonnets, covered by silk, or quilted material in winter.

The brothers' clothing also changed over the years, with the breeches and long hose of early years replaced by trousers of cotton and then linen. Jacket colors varied over the years from gray to drab to blue. Work smocks like those of men of the world were used for farming and workshop tasks.

The men's great coats and the sisters' long cloaks were greatly admired by the world's people.

As they declined in numbers, Shakers adopted more worldly dress, with lengths modified to today's fashion. The sisters today also select their own patterns and colors. However, their dress retains the lines of the early 1900s style, with the large bertha.

Some of the sisters today also retain the white cap. At Sabbathday Lake, slacks are worn for yard and garden work, and tennis shoes are accepted for hurrying about the community from job to job.

17. What was life like for Shaker children?

Children did not live in the dwellinghouses with the adult brothers and sisters. Instead, girls lived in the Girls' House with appointed caretakers and boys in the Boys' House until of an age to join the adults.

Children came to the celibate Shakers in several ways. Some had been born to Believers before their conversion. Others were orphans placed by the authorities, and some came from families that could not care for them.

School was held for the boys during the winter months and for girls in the summer. The children were taught reading, writing, spelling, arithmetic, history, physiology and geography. By 1877 children were being

taught the metric system. In more recent years subjects such as music and elocution were added. Recesses were spent doing hand work.

Seth Young Wells, who was in charge of the first city school in Albany before converting to Shakerism, was responsible for the development of much of the Shaker approach to education. The first Shaker schoolhouse was built in 1823. Shaker schools conformed to local and state laws.

Children were taught trades, working beside the brothers and sisters. Sometimes tools scaled down to fit small hands were made for the children. Just as Shaker adults were guided by the Millenial Laws, advice and guidance for children was set forth in various Shaker publications, starting with the *Juvenile Monitor* in 1823.

18. Why are things made by the Shakers so prized today?

Almost everything made by the Shakers, whether for their own use or for sale to the world's people, is highly prized by modern collectors of Americana. Private collectors, and often museums, avidly seek the Believers' furniture, tools, literature, and "smallwares" such as oval boxes, brushes and bottles.

Indeed, a small but significant Shaker economy has been created by the world's people. Several antique and Americana dealers devote themselves almost exclusively to Shaker, and auctions dedicated to Shaker items are widely advertised and heavily attended. One mail order house devotes itself entirely to selling Shaker furniture kits and other reproductions; finished and kit reproduction furniture can also be obtained from other sources. In addition to museum shops, there are several gift shops in various parts of the country specializing in items of Shaker design.

Some of the interest in Shaker things comes from their fascinating history and the unique role they have played in American life. But much of it is inspired by the superb craftsmanship and excellent design with which the Shakers consecrated everything they did. Their handwork, as author Edward Deming Andrews put it, was "religion in wood."

The beauty of Shaker furniture and other objects derives from their perfect functionalism. There is no unnecessary adornment; everything works. In this the Shakers were far ahead of their time, which may explain why so much Shaker furniture looks "modern." The Shakers themselves said it this way: "Anything may, with strict propriety, be called perfect which perfectly answers the purpose for which it was designed."

The craftsmanship which the Shakers devoted to everything they did also means that few Shaker objects can be described as crude or imperfect. There was no room for "seconds" in the Shaker way of thinking. Here, too, the Believers glorified God by achieving perfection with the work of their hands. Thomas Merton has said, "The peculiar grace of a Shaker chair is due to the fact that it was made by someone capable of believing that an angel might come and sit on it."

Shakers today are amazed at prices being paid for items that once were made simply for ordinary household chores or for sale to the world for a few dollars. The Shakers do not wish to be remembered for the objects they crafted, but the beliefs that made those objects what they were.

19. Do the Shakers accept modern things?

Perhaps because their membership peaked long ago, or perhaps because their beliefs are different than ours, we may tend to think of the Shakers as quaint, or naive and backward. Some people may also confuse them with the Amish, who do shun modern technology.

In reality, the Shakers have always been interested in modern ideas, particularly the technology useful in farming and domestic chores. They have avidly followed news of scientific devloments in these areas. The Shakers may have shunned the material culture of the world's people, but they did not shun anything that would contribute to their efficiency or the good health of their people.

During their peak years, the Shakers were very up to date — and frequently ahead of their time in farming and sanitation. In 1826 they erected the famous round stone dairy barn at Hancock, Massachusetts, a design which permitted one man working in the center of the building to feed and water the cattle with a minimum of motion. Often the Shakers installed running water or electricity before their neighbors. In about 1910 a woodshed at Hancock was remodeled to house Shaker automobiles — which, of course, were purchased for use of the society on business and not for private pleasure.

The Shakers were especially notable for their genius in inventing devices to save labor and do work better. Among the inventions credited to them are the flat household broom so widely used today, the circular saw, the common clothespin, screw propeller, double-chambered stove, turbine water wheel, a vacuum pan for condensing extracts, cut nails, the metal pen, water-repellent fabric, and an improved clothes washing machine. Even the use of electric current as a therapeutic device has been attributed to them.

If there were large communities of Shakers today, one would probably see few, if any, television sets in their dwelling houses, but there would be many computers. And in all probability the Shakers would be creating much of their own software.

IMPROVED SHAKER WASHING MACHINE,
BUILT AT SHAKER VILLAGE,
N. H.

PATENTED July 23, 1877.

20. Why did the number of Shakers decline?

From a peak estimated at about 6,000 members in 1850, the number of Shakers had declined to a handful in 1994.

People often assume the Shakers' celibacy accounts for their decline, but that is too simple an answer. In fact, a number of social and economic factors are involved.

For one, the great religious revivals from which Shakerism was able to draw so many converts died down as the nineteenth century matured, and more secular interests took their place.

With the opening of the American West, free or cheap land drew people from the East with the promise of independence and better lives. In the East itself, growing industrialization offered jobs and business opportunities to both men and women.

Women, able to find jobs, did not need the protection of communal societies. Orphans, raised by the Shakers, increasingly chose to see "the World" rather than join the Believers.

Although Shaker products, such as brooms, dried foods and preserves, were widely esteemed for their quality, they began to lose ground to mass produced goods. The Civil War damaged Shaker trade routes and Shaker assets in the South. And fewer men entering the United Society meant an added expense to the Believers for hiring outside help.

The quality and the fervor of the leadership declined as the pioneer Shakers died. Mismanagement of funds hurt many communities. Starting with Tyringham in

Massachusetts in 1875, one after another the major communities closed at a slow but inexorable pace that continued until 1960, when Hancock, near Pittsfield, Massachusetts, closed 170 years after it had opened.

Today, only one New England community remains: Sabbathday Lake in Maine.

21. Are there still Shakers today?

Yes, Shakers still live at one Shaker community: Sabbathday Lake, Maine (between Portland and Lewiston).

Established in 1794, the Sabbathday Lake community near Poland Spring is home today for several Shaker sisters and brothers.

While tourists stop to visit the museum and scholars use the library, Sabbathday Lake is still a community with work to be done. Sheep are raised, a variety of candies and herbal products are sold at the community and at fairs in Maine and Massachussets, and church services are held in the same meeting house built in 1794.

The Shakers publish the **Shaker Quarterly** for members of a support group known as "The Friends of the Shakers." The "Friends" volunteer their services during the year and especially for "Work Day" projects.

The Shakers dress simply in more modern clothing and like Shakers of the past, share in preparation of meals and housekeeping chores.

22. Do the Shakers still dance and sing?

In their earliest years, the Shakers engaged in what was called "free" dancing: uncoordinated, individual whirling and swaying. As early as the 1780s, efforts began to codify these movements into orderly patterns. At first, the worshippers simply began in two ranks, males and females facing each other, and engaged in a square-order shuffle. In 1815 hand motions accompanied with exercise songs were introduced, followed by marching two years later, and, in 1822, ring dances.

But as Shakers declined in number and the number of elderly who could not participate increased, dancing was discontinued. Occasionally today, however, Shakers may join hands and dance in a circle when they feel a meeting has become somewhat "stiff" or when, perhaps, they feel a visitor needs to be put at ease.

Singing has always been an important part of Shaker life and is today as well. The Shakers are credited with composing 10,000 songs, more than any other single group in America.

The Shaker song, "The Gift to Be Simple," came to public attention when Aaron Copeland used it in his "Appalachian Spring." Many of the verses of Shaker songs were gentle reminders for doing good or teaching humility. Many had their origins in the Scriptures and others were sung to lighten daily work. For almost every daily task or heartfelt statement of the spirit there was a Shaker tune.

For years Shaker songs were handed down by oral tradition. Later the Shakers devised a unique notation system for writing down their songs.

23. Are the Shakers worried about dying out?

At one time — the 1850s — they numbered an estimated 6,000 members in 18 major communities in states ranging from Maine to Kentucky. Today, there are only a handful of Shakers left in one New England community. Aren't they concerned that Shakerism is dying?

"Nay! Not unless God and Christ and eternal verities are failing."

That answer was uttered many years ago by Shakers Anna White and Leila S. Taylor.

Spiritual life, they explained, moves in spirals. There is always a period of decline between the passing of the old and the coming of the new. Even as Shakerism seems to be ebbing, its influence may be advancing in some other manner.

This is possible because the "elastic nature" of Shaker faith permits it to "receive the impress of newly revealed truth and expand in new forms."

So as one era of Shakerism may be ending, the Shakers believe, another may be underway, though in another shape.

Several years ago Sister R. Mildred Barker of Sabbathday Lake told members of a historical society in Ohio:

"Shakerism is no failure. It is good, and therefore of God, and no good is ever a failure.

"The principals and ideals which the Shakers were the first to expound have gone out into the world and, like a pebble dropped in the water, we cannot measure the distance of the influence they have borne . . .

"Shakerism is not dying out, nor is it a failure."

Directory of
Interesting Sites

KENTUCKY
Shaker Village of Pleasant Hill

You can sleep in authentic Shaker buildings and dine on hearty Kentucky fare in this meticulously restored village in the quiet countryside near Lexington. This is America's only National Historic Landmark with all guest services in original buildings. A Shaker village from 1806 to 1910, Pleasant Hill was reopened as a museum in 1968 and now preserves 33 original buildings.

Location: On U.S. 68, 25 miles southwest of Lexington and 7 miles northeast of Harrodsburg, Ky.

Open: Year around, except Christmas Eve and Christmas Day.

For More Information and Reservations: Write: Shakertown at Pleasant Hill, 3501 Lexington Rd., Harrodsburg, KY 40330 or call (800) 734-5611. Website: www. ShakerVillageKy.org.

Shaker Museum at South Union

Founded in 1807, this was the longest-lived of the seven western Shaker societies, and the last of them to close (1922). Today the museum offers four buildings, including its majestic Centre House, filled with original Shaker furniture and crafts. The museum also owns the 1869 Shaker Tavern and the 1917 Store, housing the South Union post office—in continuous operation since 1826.

Location: On U.S. 68 between Bowling Green and Auburn, in southwestern Kentucky.

Open: Daily March 1 through December 1.

For More Information: Write Shaker Museum at South Union, KY 42283, or call (502) 542-4167. E-mail: shakermus@logantele.com. Website: www.logantele.com/~shakmus/.

MAINE

Sabbathday Lake

Founded in 1794, this is still a living, working Shaker community. Sheep and herbs are raised here, research into Shaker history continues, and restoration of the village goes on. Walking tours, exhibits, and shops are open to visitors. Sabbathday Lake's herb business today dates back to the early years of the community, when it was known as West Gloucester. Special events information, herb catalog and Shaker Press folder available on request.

Location: SR 26, 8 miles north of Gray, 12 miles south of Auburn.

Open: Memorial Day through Columbus Day, Monday through Saturday. The Shaker Library is open year-round for research; appointments required.

For More Information: Write The United Society of Shakers, 707 Shaker Rd., New Gloucester, ME 04260 or call (207) 926-4597.

MASSACHUSETTS
Fruitlands Museums

The 1794 Shaker House is one of four separate museums at
Fruitlands, a delightful collection of Americana in a beautiful
hillside setting. The Shaker building was originally used as an office
by the nearby Harvard society of Believers, which flourished from
1791 to 1918, and was moved here in 1920. Shaker furniture and a
wide range of handicrafts are on display in the Shaker House.

Location: On Prospect Hill Road in the town of Harvard, 2 ¼ miles
south of Route 2. From Route 2 take Route 110 south, turn right
onto Old Shirley Road, and follow signs.

Open: Mid-May through Mid-October, seven days a week.

For More Information: Write Fruitlands Museums, 102 Prospect
Hill Rd., Harvard, MA 01451, or call (978) 456-3924.

Hancock Shaker Village

"The City of Peace," as the Shakers called Hancock, was settled
in 1790 and is a living history museum of Shaker life, crafts and
farming. Set on 1,200 scenic acres, Hancock says it is the most
extensive of the restored Shaker villages and that it houses the
largest collection of Shaker furniture and artifacts at an original
site. Rural life in primarily the 18th and 19th centuries is presented
through an interactive, dynamic program of presentations, talks,
tours and demonstrations. Hancock Shaker Village is also an
historic working farm with heritage breeds of livestock and
heirloom vegetable gardens.

Location: Just past the junction of Routes 20 and 41, in Pittsfield,
Massachusetts

Open: Daily April–November.

For More Information: Write Hancock Shaker Village, P.O. Box
927, Pittsfield, MA 01202, or call (800) 817-1137.
E-mail: info@hancockshakervillage.org.
Website: www.hancockshakervillage.org.

NEW HAMPSHIRE
Canterbury Shaker Village

Organized in 1792, the historical community includes 24 buildings set amidst beautiful countryside. Guided walking tours of six buildings and daily craft demonstrations, herb garden and three self-guided nature trails including mill sites available. The Creamery Restaurant serves Shaker-inspired meals. The Shaker Village Gift Shop features Shaker and handcrafted gifts, reproduction furniture and books and tapes.

Location: North of Concord, N.H. North or southbound I-93 travelers use exit 18, follow signs to the village.

Open: Daily, including holidays, May-October. Nov. & Dec., Friday, Saturday and Sunday.

For More Information: Write Canterbury Shaker Village, 288 Shaker Road, Canterbury, NH 03224, or call (603) 783-9511.

Enfield Shaker Museum

In 1793 the pioneer Believers moved to the west shore of Mascoma Lake and were formally organized as the Enfield Society of Shakers. Membership eventually reached over 300 but dwindled to 8 by 1923 and the society was dissolved. The Great Stone Dwelling House, built in 1837, was the largest of the Shaker dwelling structures, and today is operated as an inn and restaurant where guests can sleep and dine in the same rooms the Shakers occupied beginning in 1841.

Location: In west-central New Hampshire near Hanover. Take Exit 17 off Route 89, follow 4 East to 4A South and follow the signs. Admission.

Open: Museum, exhibits, garden open daily from June 1 to mid-October.

For More Information: Write Enfield Shaker Museum, 2 Lower Shaker Village, Enfield, NH 03748; or call (603) 632-4346. E-mail: chosen.vale@valley.net. Website: www.valley.net/~esm.

NEW YORK
Mount Lebanon Shaker Village

From the 1780s until 1947 the Shakers built a complex village consisting of more than 130 buildings and more than a dozen mill ponds on 8,000 acres. Divided into eight "families," several thousand Shakers lived here and 1,000 are buried here. The first community organized, it was a model for all others and as the Central Ministry served as the headquarters of the Shaker Church. Twenty-four original Shaker buildings and more than 72 acres of land are owned by the Mount Lebanon Shaker Village, a non-profit educational institution. Darrow School occupies several buildings. Others are open to the public or await restoration. Slide presentation, exhibits and guided tours are available.

Location: New Lebanon, N.Y., 25 miles east of Albany and 8 miles west of Pittsfield, Mass., off U.S. 20 on Darrow Rd.

Open: Memorial Day through Labor Day, Saturday and Sunday.

For More Information: Write Mount Lebanon Shaker Village, Shaker Road, P.O. Box 628, New Lebanon, NY 12125, or call (518) 794-9500.

The Shaker Museum and Library at Old Chatham

One of the largest and most comprehensive Shaker collections is housed in an exquisite country setting. With more than 7,500 items exhibited in 26 display areas, the Museum and Library reflects over 200 years of Shaker history through interpretive exhibitions of furniture, tools and machinery, handcrafted materials, textiles, and inventions. The object collection is enhanced with the archival holdings. The object collection is enhanced with the archival holdings of the Emma B. King Library. The Museum Shop and Summer Cafe, featuring Shaker-related publications and reproduction items, is open during regular exhibition hours.

Location: On Shaker Museum Road, off County Route 13, one mile south of Old Chatham, N.Y. The museum is 35 minutes from Albany and 3 hours from New York City or Boston.

Open: Daily except Tuesday—May 1-October 31. (Library—year round by appointment).

For More Information: Write The Shaker Museum and Library, Old Catham, NY 12136 or call (518) 794-9100.

NEW YORK
Watervliet

America's first Shaker settlement (1776), Watervliet was an active Shaker site from 1776 until 1938. Even before that Mother Ann used the site as her base of operations and is buried in the Watervliet Shaker Cemetery. Today the Shaker Heritage society is working to develop the site. The 1848 Meeting House, the Shaker orchard, and the graveyard where Mother Ann is buried are open to the public.

Location: Adjacent to Albany International Airport, west of Adirondack Northway (I-87) exit 4, a few miles north of New York Thruway exit 24 on the grounds of the Ann Lee Health Facility.

Open: Tuesday-Saturday.

For More Information: Write Shaker Heritage Society, 1848 Shaker Meeting House, Albany-Shaker Road, Albany, NY 12211, or call (518) 456-7890. E-mail: shakerwv@crisny.org. Fax: (518) 452-7348.

OHIO

The Golden Lamb, Lebanon

In continuous operation since 1803 and Ohio's oldest inn, The Golden Lamb has been host to Mark Twain, Charles Dickens, Ulysses S. Grant, and 10 other United States Presidents. All 18 overnight room are furnished in antiques and named after a famous guest. Two Shaker display rooms are on the fourth floor. Shaker furniture is used throughout the Gift Shop and Public Room. The Golden Lamb is located in historic Lebanon, a town older than the state of Ohio. The Shaker society of Union Village (1805-1910) was located near here.

Location: 27 South Broadway at the intersection of Ohio routes 63 and 123. From I-75, exit at Ohio 63 and follow signs. From I-71 exit Ohio 48, three miles north to Lebanon.

Open: Throughout the year, except Christmas Day.

For More Information: Write The Golden Lamb, 27 S. Broadway, Lebanon, OH 45036 or call (513) 932-5065.

Kettering-Moraine Museum

Administered on behalf of the Dayton suburbs of Kettering and Moraine, the Kettering-Moraine Museum preserves local history, including that of the nearby Watervliet (Ohio) Shaker community society (1806-1900.) At one time Watervliet was the publishing center of the western Shaker societies.

In addition to furniture and artifacts from Watervliet and other Shaker villages, the Miller's House has been moved here from Watervliet. The Shaker Tannery Barn also has been moved here and opened to the public.

Location: 35 Moraine Circle South in Kettering.

Open: Sunday afternoons.

For More Information: Write Kettering-Moraine Museum, 35 Moraine Circle South, Kettering, OH 45438, or call (937) 299-2722.

OHIO

Shaker Historical Museum, Shaker Heights

The North Union Shaker Society was founded near Cleveland in 1822. Once referred to as "The Valley of God's Pleasure," North Union was closed in 1889, and later was razed for one of America's first planned suburbs, Shaker Heights. Today, the Shaker Historical Museum is housed in a 1910 mansion constructed by the enterprising Van Sweringen brothers, developers of Shaker Heights. Overlooking Horse Shoe Lake, the museum's front yard was once part of the Center Family's apple orchard.

Location: 16740 South Park Blvd., Shaker Heights. Exit I-271 at Chargin Blvd., turn left, follow Chargin Blvd. west, turn right on Lee Road, and right on South Park Blvd.

Open: 2-5 Tuesday-Friday and Sundays.

For More Information: Write The Shaker Historical Society, 16740 South Park Blvd., Shaker Heights, OH 44120, or call (216) 921-1201. Fax: (216) 921-2615. E-mail: shakehist@wviz.org. Website: www.cwru.edu/affil/shakhist/shaker.htm.

Warren County Historical Society Museum

The Shaker community at Union Village (1805-1912) was located near here, at Turtle Creek. Union Village, which at its peak had an estimated 600 members, was considered the parent organization of Shaker societies in the southwest. Among other things, Union Village became known for its skill in making palm-leaf bonnets. The historical society calls the Shaker collection in its museum the largest in the Midwest. The newly completed Robert H. and Virginia Jones Shaker Gallery includes seven rooms.

Location: 105 South Broadway, Lebanon, Ohio near the intersection of Ohio 63, 48 and 123.

Open: Daily except Mondays and holidays.

Admission: Adults $3.00; students through high school, $1.00

For More Information: Write the Warren County Historical Society Museum, 105 South Broadway, Lebanon, OH 45036, or call (513) 932-1817. E-mail: WCHS@compuserve.com.

ALSO WORTH NOTING

DELAWARE

Winterthur Museum, Winerthur, DE 19735; telephone
(800) 448-3883. Two rooms of Shaker furnishings. Web site:
www.winterthur.org.

KENTUCKY

Kentucky Museum, U.S. 68 on Western Kentucky University
Campus, Bowling Green, KY 42101; telephone (502) 745-2592.
South Union Shaker furniture, tools, crafts, manuscripts.

NEW YORK

Metropolitan Museum of Art, Fifth Avenue at 82nd St., New York,
NY 10028; telephone (212) 879-5500. Shaker retiring room on
permanent exhibit in American wing.

OHIO

Western Reserve Historical Society, 10825 East Blvd., Cleveland,
OH 44106; telephone (216) 721-5722. World's lar gest collection
of Shaker research materials.

PENNSYLVANIA

Philadelphia Museum of Art, Benjamin Franklin Parkway at 26th
St., Philadelphia, PA 19130; telephone (215) 763-8100. Sister's
room, exhibit of Shaker furniture, artifacts. Web site:
www.philamuseum.org.

VERMONT

Shelburne Museum, U.S. 7, south of Burlington, VT, in Shelburne,
VT 05482; telephone (802) 985-3344. A c. 1834-1853 Shaker Horse
Stand and Storage Building from Canterbury, N.H., renovated and
restored and housing tools, household implements, woodworking
tool collection and other Shaker artifacts. Open daily late May to
late October.

THE SHAKER MESSENGER

Retail Store Featuring
Shaker and Folk Art

When in Holland, Mich., plan to visit The Shaker Messenger—a retail store operated by Diana Van Kolken featuring Shaker reproductions and American Folk Art by craftspersons met during the past 18 years. In a gallery setting, many of the items are one-of-a-kind. We are located in downtown Holland which has undergone a multi-million dollar renovation complete with a snowmelt system beneath the sidewalks and streets.

Hours are Mon., Thurs., and Fri. 10-9; Tue., Wed. and Sat. 10-5:30; Sunday noon-5.

Gallery located at 210 S. River Ave.
Phone (616) 396-4588 FAX (616) 396-3467

The Shaker Messenger P.O. Box 45 Holland, MI 49423

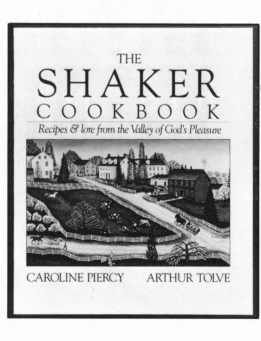